Sagittarius

22 November – 20 December

amber
BOOKS

ASTROLOGICAL SIGN DATES:

The precise start and end times for each sign vary by a day or two from year to year as the Gregorian calendar shifts relative to the tropical year. The dates provided in this book are correct for the year 2020.

If you are unsure of the Zodiac sign for your specific birth year, visit: www.yourzodiacsign.com.

Sagittarius

22 November – 20 December

A guide to understanding yourself, your friendships and finding your true love

This edition first published in 2020 by
Amber Books Ltd
United House
North Road
London N7 9DP
United Kingdom
www.amberbooks.co.uk
Instagram: amberbooksltd
Facebook: amberbooks
Twitter: @amberbooks

ISBN: 978-1-83886-032-5

Project Editor: Sarah Uttridge
Design: Zoë Mellors

Picture Credits:
All illustrations by Fabbri Publications except the following:
Shutterstock: 31 (Elena Naumchenkova), 32 (La Puma), 35 (Slonomysh), 40 (Angel Soler Gollonet)

Printed and bound in China

TRADITIONAL CHINESE BOOKBINDING

This book has been produced using traditional Chinese bookbinding techniques, using a method that was developed during the Ming Dynasty (1368–1644) and remained in use until the adoption of Western binding techniques in the early 1900s. In traditional Chinese binding, single sheets of paper are printed on one side only, and each sheet is folded in half, with the printed pages on the outside. The book block is then sandwiched between two boards and sewn together through punched holes close to the cut edges of the folded sheets.

Contents

Introduction

Sagittarius

22 November–20 December

Sign: The Archer or Centaur
Ruling Planet: Jupiter
Gender: Masculine
Element: Fire
Quality: Mutable
Compatibility: Aquarius and Libra
Non-compatibility: Cancer, Scorpio and Taurus

Every man, woman and child is born with a distinct and different destiny. There are no exceptions. Everyone has cosmic significance and a part to play in the life of the universe. This is innate and inescapable, and goes beyond the tiny boundaries of nation, creed and colour.

As we live out our lives on planet Earth, we are, however unknowingly, acting in a greater drama and reacting to impulses that come from distant astronomical bodies, stars and planets millions of light years away. Sceptics pour scorn on the idea that far-distant Saturn, for example, can have any effect on our lives, as the ancient art and science of astrology teaches. But the fact is that we are sparks of energy inhabiting bodies made of the same stuff as the stars, responding like tiny radios to the distant messages they send to Earth.

Each infant carries within it a double blueprint for life: its genetic programming and the pattern of character that comes from the astrological 'clock' that was set in motion at the moment of birth. No one knows the full extent of genetic influence, although it seems to be astonishingly far-reaching, but the power of the horoscope has been well known to the wisest men and women for many centuries.

Our Sun and Moon signs provide essential inside information about our destinies. They reveal the secrets of who we really are, and why we are here, laying out before us our potential, the sort of joys and achievements our characteristics may bring about, and warn us of problems to be overcome through the triumph of free will.

Read this book with an open mind and discover who you really are.

The Elements

Up to the beginning of the Age of Enlightenment – the modern scientific era – in the 18th century, it was commonly believed that everything, including human beings, was made up of the four elements: Earth, Air, Fire and Water. These were thought of as the building blocks of life, and each astrological sign had a predominance of one or another. Each created its common characteristics, although too much of any of the elements can produce an unbalanced personality.

Fire Signs

The Fire signs are Aries, Leo and Sagittarius. Consumed with passion – which all too often, however, takes the form of self-love and burning ambition – these are the natural stars of the zodiac. They are fired up with motivation, and sparks really fly when they get going. It is difficult to keep a Fire sign doing things at a measured pace (steady old Taureans can sometimes do it, though) because their enthusiasms soon spread like wildfire, catching the imaginations of more and more people. Fire signs are the leaders – especially Leo, the most regal and imperious of all the signs of the zodiac.

Fire signs do, nevertheless, have great warmth and charisma, and light the way for others to follow. Arians can burn with a cold flame or with the raging fires of revolution. Either way, their passion is based on a childlike – even childish – desire to get their own way, without any thought for the future or the feelings of others. But they are willing to go where others fear to tread, and without them human progress would always be a great deal slower and more difficult.

Sagittarians are the great enthusiasts of the zodiac, sparky and constantly generating yet more energy. Like the centaur-archer and the horse-man of their sign, Sagittarians can rush into things, galloping at the gate that is never going to open at the last minute, or shooting wide of the mark. But they will pick themselves up and start again, uncomplainingly, forever encouraging more timid souls, while keeping their own eyes on new horizons.

Fire Signs
Aries
Leo
Sagittarius

Colours of the Zodiac

Traditionally, each sign of the zodiac has its own colour, which is believed to be 'lucky' or magically empowered for those born under that particular sign. In general, the colours are associated with the ruling planets and are symbolic of their attributes. Many people find that they feel most comfortable when wearing their sign's colours, and often choose them without knowing their full astrological background.

Sagittarius

Ruling Planet: Jupiter.

Colours: Dark blue and purple.

Expansive, luxury-loving and gregarious Jupiter also has a regal streak – hence the royal colour purple. Although sometimes a difficult colour to wear, it can bestow dignity.

The Angelic Hierarchy

According to ancient tradition, each planet is governed by one of the great archangels, who are also rulers of certain aspects of human life. The box below lists the planet that they rule, the areas over which they have influence and their special day of the week.

Sachiel

Archangel of Jupiter.

Governs: Sagittarius.

Rules: Financial gain, windfalls and material luck.

Day: Thursday.

The Genders

Traditionally, the twelve signs of the zodiac are divided into Masculine and Feminine, although of course both men and women are born into each.

The characteristics were assigned to the genders aeons ago, well before modern feminism or political correctness, and may now seem old-fashioned to many. However, the signs do seem to be grouped according to the appropriate gender.

The Masculine Signs

The Masculine signs are Aries, Gemini, Leo, Libra, Sagittarius and Aquarius. Masculine traits do tend to be accentuated in the Fire signs, which are Aries, Leo and Sagittarius.

Masculine signs are dominant and assertive, often to the point of being pugnacious and extroverted. They are natural leaders and rulers, showing fiery initiative, and are fiercely protective of others in their care. They are pioneers and visionaries, conquerors of new lands and the first to achieve great things. They tend to tackle things themselves and can be impatient with others who are less assertive.

Negatively, Masculine signs can be egotistical, arrogant and cruel, and dismissive of the needs and feelings of others. They can often prove to be troublemakers and rebels – violent, belligerent and inclined to subversion.

The Ruling Planets

Until the 18th century, astrologers knew only the planets of our solar system that could be seen with the naked eye: Mercury, Venus, Mars, Jupiter and Saturn. (For the purposes of astrology, the Sun and the Moon are also counted as planets even though the Sun is a star and the Moon is the satellite of Earth.) Uranus was discovered in 1781, Neptune in 1846 and Pluto was first seen in 1930. Many astrologers believe that the existence of other heavenly bodies – such as the rumoured Vulcan, which hypothetically exists within the orbit of Mercury – is about to be confirmed. Astrologers will then have to agree which signs these 'new' planets will rule, and what human characteristics their discovery will accentuate.

Jupiter

Jupiter has 16 moons, two of which, Ganymede and Callisto, were discovered by the Italian astronomer Galileo Galilei in 1610. Jupiter naturally emits radio waves, which have confused and temporarily excited beyond compare amateur astronomers who frequently think they have finally made contact with extra-terrestrial beings.

Jupiter was the Greco-Roman god of plenty – also known as Jove or, in ancient Greece, Zeus. He was the protecting father-god of the city of Rome. The Egyptians had no god of plenty, but sometimes the Earth god, Geb, and Ptah, the father-god, were worshipped for their beneficence. In many cultures it was the fertile Earth Mother who bestowed all material blessings on her children, so the seasons of the year became associated with her waxing and waning fecundity.

Traditionally deemed a 'lucky' planet by astrologers, Jupiter is the ruler of Sagittarius, and is

About Jupiter

A far-distant 778 million km (484 million miles) from the Sun, the planet Jupiter measures a massive 145,000 km (90,000 million miles) across. It is the largest heavenly body in our solar system, although much of its mass is composed of hydrogen and helium.

Jupiter's sacred day is Thursday.

associated with joy, plenty, philosophy and all manner of academic study. Happy-go-lucky and naturally disposed to be optimistic, Sagittarians do seem to embody the air of cheerful expectancy conjured up by the image of Jupiter. They accept that anything can happen but have little fear for the future, feeling instinctively that fate will take care of them, and it usually does. Sagittarians are often happiest with their head buried in a book.

The Qualities

In addition to the influence of gender, the elements and the planets, each sign of the zodiac is affected by having an intrinsic quality – Cardinal, Fixed or Mutable.

Mutable Quality

Those born under the Mutable signs are always on the move, either physically or mentally, forever seeking fresh fields and pastures new. They are restless, versatile and flexible, hating routine and any form of strict discipline. These individuals can have butterfly minds, endlessly alighting on new enthusiasms, fads or crazes, then dropping them just as quickly and moving on to the next thing. Mutable people can be unreliable and irresponsible, and are rarely self-disciplined, although they are often extremely charming.

Sagittarius

Always on the move, always with an eye to the next project, lover or ambition, Sagittarians are very Mutable individuals. They become unhappy, sometimes to the point of becoming ill, if they are restricted or expected to conform. Sagittarians are delightful people with unbounded energy and a relentless curiosity about life, but they frequently lack the energy necessary to follow projects through to their conclusion.

Signs and Symbols

Most people are familiar with the zodiac 'zoo' – the collection of symbols that represent the twelve signs. These images reflect the characteristics traditionally assigned to each sign and contain a wealth of knowledge about its true nature.

Each sign of the zodiac is represented by a symbol – the twin fish for Pisces, for example. No one is sure exactly when or why the symbols were chosen, although some authorities believe they date from Sumeria or Mesopotamia, 4000 years before Jesus Christ. The priest-astrologers of the ancient world were the first to impose recognizable patterns on the great constellations – Leo the Lion being one example.

Today, seeing such shapes in the stars may seem fanciful, but thousands of years ago imaginations were more poetic, and many myths told of magical animals, such as the dragon, which had strange powers to influence everyday human life.

Although the ancient Egyptians left few astrological records, they were almost unique in antiquity for worshipping archetypal, animal-headed gods. However, these strange hybrid gods – half-human, half-animal – were worshipped as aspects of one God. Contrary to the general belief that the Egyptians were idolaters, their religion was basically monotheistic. Each statue represented an aspect of the one true God.

Since they were established, the signs have remained unchanged, although there was a movement in the Middle Ages to change the sign of Aquarius to the sign of John the Baptist – presumably because of the connection with water.

The twelve signs of the zodiac do seem particularly apt on the whole, and accurately reflect the archetypal character of Sun sign types. The great Swiss psychoanalyst Carl Gustav Jung (1875–1961) believed that, deep in our psyches, humanity shares a collective unconscious – a set of archetypal images, which, at a profound level, we all understand. The signs of the zodiac form part of this pool of images, conveying eternal truths to our unconscious minds.

Signs and Symbols

Sagittarius The Archer or Centaur

The Archer was the mainstay of ancient armies. Poised, strong-armed and alert, with his eye constantly on the far-distant target, the arrows flew swiftly from his bow. Although some of them may have fallen short, many hit the bull's-eye – rather like the myriad ideas and ambitions of a typical Sagittarian.

Energy, virility and even a certain dream-like surrealism distinguish the symbol of the Centaur – who is often also shown with bow and arrow. The Centaurs were ubiquitous in Greek mythology, where they were often depicted as being particularly sexually voracious. For example, in the story of the rape of the Sabine women by the early Romans, it is the Centaurs who carried off the women.

Sometimes Centaurs were associated with Pan, the hooved nature god of the ancient world, whose musical pipes could lure the unwary into the deepest woods. There, they would become so disoriented that panic ensued. Indeed, this is where our word 'panic' derives from. Pan was also linked with unashamed sexuality, and his statues were often depicted with erect phallae. In ancient Egypt, he was known as Min, who was also shown as ithyphallic.

Pan was believed to have been killed off by the coming of Christianity. One story tells how a mysterious voice could be heard moaning 'Pan is dead!' – but the modern pagan movement, both in Europe and the United States, has seen a return to his worship and a newed respect for nature.

The Sun in Sagittarius

Sun sign Sagittarians are some of the most likeable folk around: open, optimistic, enthusiastic and tolerant. Their ruler, Jupiter, is traditionally supposed to be lucky, and this largest of all the planets in the solar system does seem to bestow very positive opportunities on Sagittarians. Possibly this is because their attitude actively invites such opportunity. Exuberant and often restless, Sagittarians are adept at inspiring and encouraging more pessimistic and cautious souls, although they can be foolhardy, getting into worrying situations. Usually, though, they get out without much trouble.

Many people born under the sign of the Archer find it hard to concentrate for very long on any one subject unless it captures their imagination, and then they can give their whole selves to it for hours. Their keen and restless minds are always looking to the future, trying to be one jump ahead – and often succeeding in being at least two. The joyful Sagittarians have an infectious joy and curiosity, and are an interesting blend of the studious – happy to sit with their books for long periods of time, totally oblivious to the outside world – and the very physical, for they are essentially outdoor types. No wonder then that many astrologers believe Australia to be the ideal Sagittarian country.

Sagittarians are also inclined to philosophy and religion, although they rarely become bigots or fanatics. They love discussing their ideas, often late into the night, and are happy to share their home with a large number of very diverse people as well as animals, of whom they are very fond.

Personality traits of Sagittarians

Positive	*Negative*
Optimistic	Unsettled
Enthusiastic	Irresponsible
Tolerant	Gamblers
Open	Foolhardy
Studious	Short attention span
Likeable	Blindly optimistic
Independent	Aloof
Exuberant	Impulsive

However, excessive Sagittarian energy can be disconcerting. People born under this sign tend to flit from job to job, from lover to lover and from home to home. Some may never settle, remaining life's nomads to the very end. Most Sagittarians are natural backpackers at some point in their lives. Other people may find this restlessness disturbing, especially the more staid, security-minded materialists, such as Taurus or Virgo, whose home is their castle. They fail to understand why anyone would want to leave it. Sagittarians tend to see their home as more of a tent that they fold, metaphorically, before leaving for their latest adventure.

Sagittarians can take this footloose and fancy-free attitude much too far, though. It can easily degenerate into mindless optimism and irresponsibility, and make them rely on impossible scenarios to get them out of trouble. They make compulsive gamblers, seeing Lady Luck constantly beckoning. Others may try to tell them she is merely a mirage, but to Sagittarians she is tantamount to a religious vision.

Appearance

Sagittarians come in several types, including the super-athletic. The men can have wide shoulders and a slim waist and hips, while the women may be bronzed and muscular. They have quick, determined mannerisms and daring, piercing eyes that are always likely to flash with laughter. While not particularly fashion-conscious, Sagittarians can look trendy. Whatever their age, they favour youthful styles, but take care to add their own personal touch to each ensemble. Some Sagittarians are rather eccentric and convey bizarre first impressions.

Health

With such unbounded energy, Sagittarians often fail to look before they leap and, as a result, suffer quite a few bruises, pulled muscles and broken bones. What they need to do is channel and balance their mental, physical

and spiritual energies. Many find yoga, Tai Chi and meditation of great benefit. Sometimes, they even become teachers of these arts. Sagittarians need to feel that they are in control of their minds and bodies, and like to plan an exercise regime and diet that is right for them. Some, however, may be totally unconcerned with what they eat and drink. They will happily refuel on any old junk food, but most, especially in later years, take an interest in healthy eating. Some can even become health-food bores. Conversely, Sagittarians can throw themselves with typical abandon into the hedonistic life, feasting on rich, fatty foods and drinking too much beer, which they love. However, all they normally need to change to a healthier lifestyle is sound advice from a doctor or someone else they respect.

Traditionally, the hips and thighs are problem areas for Sagittarians. Perhaps all that distinctive twisting and twirling puts a strain on them. So it is a good idea to have physiotherapy or osteopathy at the first sign of trouble.

Career

Sagittarians go for anything that gives free rein to their adventurous spirits. They will never persist with any job that limits them, so they don't go far in large corporations or the civil service, where there are too many rules and regulations, and where they find it hard to express their individuality. Similarly, dull claustrophobic offices make Sagittarians feel uncomfortable. While rarely truly ambitious, Sagittarians like to see the fruits of their labours, and enjoy being appreciated. Sometimes they will rise to the top of their chosen profession without much effort. Making money is usually of secondary importance to Sagittarians. They are not seriously materialistic, and although they enjoy a few home comforts and the freedom that money can bring, on the whole their working lives are focused on deeper matters. Many find fulfilment in study, becoming life-long students or university teachers, or they take up bookish pursuits in their spare time. Sagittarians make excellent publishers. They love the look and feel of books, as well as their content – and some even set up their own generally successful publishing companies. However, typical Sun sign Sagittarians can be far too restless and disorganized to spend months, perhaps even years, actually writing a book. They would need a very efficient and diplomatic literary agent on hand to constantly support and nag them. Even then, they could miss the deadline by months.

Many Sagittarians lack staying power. They have wonderfully inspired ideas that they fully intend to turn into a concrete result, but in a very short space

The best careers for Sagittarians

- University lecturer
- Publisher
- Vicar
- Osteopath
- Athlete
- Writer
- Professional horse rider
- Entrepreneur

of time they forget all about it, become disillusioned, and turn their attention to the next tempting project. Sagittarians need to be brought down to earth gently, and can work well with the right sort of tactful, organized business partner, especially one who gives them space to be themselves.

Another area in which Sagittarians traditionally shine is religion. Many a sleepy village has been rudely awakened by the arrival of the new Sagittarian vicar, with his or her new-broom style, energy and idealism. Even when the more conventional parishioners do their best to clip the wings of these bumptious newcomers, the Sagittarians will continue to bring a breath of fresh air into their lives, whether they like it or not. Apart from the pastoral aspect of their vocation, Sagittarians find ministering to the more spiritual needs of their flock very congenial, and enjoy theological study and discussion. They tend to be keen on ecumenical movements, comparative religion, and anything that encourages greater tolerance between different faiths or lifestyles.

Often their religious bent is combined with a desire to help their fellow man. They may be hands-on healers – naturopaths, osteopaths and the like – or spiritualist mediums. Some are keen psychical researchers, travelling great distances to investigate ghosts and poltergeists, and are rarely frightened by even the most dramatic cases of things that go bump in the night. Once they have fully researched the case, Sagittarians will give powerful, inspirational talks to packed audiences and great acclaim.

Traditionally, Sagittarians makes excellent sportspeople, and many make it to the top, although they do need the strong guiding hand of a tough coach. They need to be disciplined and made to follow a regular training routine, or all that energy will be dissipated and their talent frittered away.

Sagittarians often love horses, and in fact most animals. They find great fulfilment in equestrian sports, either as keen amateurs or as professionals. In some respects, they are rather similar to these big, nervy and powerful animals, and can easily form a strong, lasting bond with them. Sagittarians are natural horse whisperers.

Relationships

Since Sagittarius is a Fire sign, people born under it are highly sexed, and have no time for prudishness or conventional attitudes.

However, they can be considerably less keen on settling down for life with one partner, and tend to take their time deciding which of their many paramours is their soulmate. Some never decide, and go blowing off through life happily solo, but always surrounded by a large circle of lovers, friends and admirers. As free spirits, Sagittarians need very understanding partners, who can cope with abrupt changes of plan. Often those born under the sign of the Centaur need to gallop off to fresh fields and pastures new, if only for a few days, to recharge their batteries. More often than not, they will want to be alone while doing it. Restless and claustrophobic, they cannot bear any form of restriction, and often react angrily when their chosen lifestyle is challenged, or when their partner demands to accompany them on their adventures.

On the whole, Sagittarians are not good at marriage, even though there are some who seek to spend all their time with the one love of their life. Many more content themselves with being serially monogamous, perfectly faithful to their partner until it is time to move on.

Many Sagittarians, on the other hand, prefer to live alone, cheerfully surrounded by the chaos of solo living, but very much at the centre of a busy social and love life. They enjoy it when friends, family and lovers drop by.

Basically, Sagittarians are good, kind people who hate unpleasantness and injustice. Any disharmony in the home or elsewhere distresses them, and often the only way they can cope with it is by running away. This tendency makes them unpredictable in relationships, and rather feckless and unreliable parents, although they can be hugely popular with children because they are very childlike themselves.

Ideal Partner

Most Sagittarians prefer to have a range of partners, chosen from all signs of the zodiac, but when they do settle down, they need to spend their lives, with easy-going, tolerant but organized people who make few demands and

who are not particularly jealous or possessive. This is something of a tall order, but certain Aquarians and Librans fit the bill. Those who are definitely not compatible with Sagittarians are weepy, clinging, insecure Cancerians, dark, intense manipulative Scorpians, and reactionary, jealous Taureans.

Compatibility in Relationships

Aries

20 March–19 April

Aries will usually try to dominate fellow Fire sign Sagittarius, which will only drive them further away.

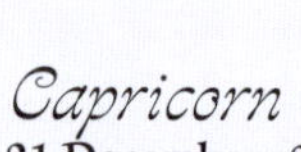

Capricorn

21 December–20 January

Sagittarians find Goats hard to understand. Their caution is anathema to the untamed Sagittarian spirit.

Cancer

21 June–21 July

The famous Cancerian compassion and talent for home-making is wasted on these free spirits.

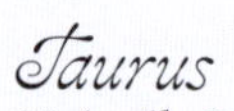

Taurus

20 April–20 May

Tame, conventional Taureans often prove too stodgy for idiosyncratic and sometimes eccentric Sagittarians.

Libra

23 September–22 October

Librans and Sagittarians are a good match, inspiring and supporting each other. Physically very compatible.

Leo

22 July–22 August

The Leonine energy and verve is attractive to fiery Sagittarius, but sooner or later they will clash.

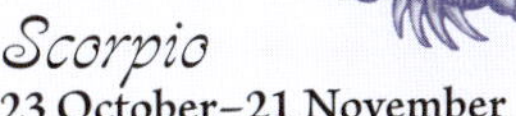

Scorpio
23 October–21 November

Dark Scorpians often try to ensnare charming Sagittarians, but intense physicality doesn't mean enduring love.

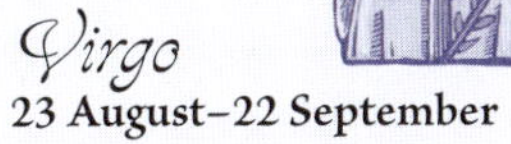

Virgo
23 August–22 September

Steady, organized and repressed, Virgoans are the complete opposite of unrealistic Sagittarians.

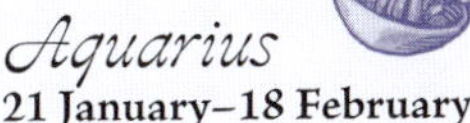

Aquarius
21 January–18 February

This can be the perfect match. Both signs have little regard for the establishment or convention.

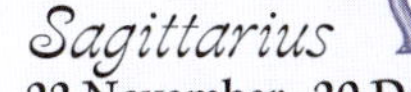

Sagittarius
22 November–20 December

Fellow Sagittarians will get on well and fuel each other's madcap schemes. Romantic, yes. Practical, no.

Gemini
21 May–20 June

Superficially on the same wavelength, but Geminians play too many games for innocent Sagittarians.

Pisces
19 February–19 March

Sagittarians have little time for self-indulgent scenes, so touchy Pisceans are unlikely to make good life partners.

The Sagittarian Child

Sun sign Sagittarian children can be a strange mix of oddball and sporty. Inquisitive, charming, quick-witted and active, they can seem like a dream to teachers or parents, but there is an underlying insecurity and waywardness in them, which can cause problems.

They find the restrictions of school an immense bore, and can resort to playing truant simply to escape into the fresh air. Although their concentration is good when their interest is fully engaged, Sagittarian children can find it hard to focus on less congenial subjects and need a firm hand with their studies. Often they don't see the point of pursuing their education beyond the normal span of around 11 years, and yearn to travel the world, experience other lifestyles and meet as many diverse people as they can. Yet once they have had their fill of travel and discovery, Sagittarians will happily sign on for a further education course, or throw themselves into a studious hobby such as local history research.

Sagittarians can be eccentric, which marks them out from their peers. However, they can charm their way out of potential bullying, and their prowess at sport is a good deterrent to anyone who thinks they must be wimps just because they like reading.

Happy-go-lucky Sagittarians feel very uncomfortable with emotional intensity or cruelty, whether directed at themselves or at others. They cannot cope with the typical Cancerian possessiveness and melodrama, nor with heavy-handed brutality, whether physical or verbal.

Famous Sagittarians

Uri Geller

Steven Spielberg

George Eliot

Louisa M. Alcott

Jane Austen

Catherine of Breganza

Walt Disney

Charles Chaplin

Winston Churchill

Joseph Conrad

Benjamin Disraeli

Bruce Lee

Edith Piaf

Ludwig von Beethoven

Jimi Hendrix

William Blake

Henri Toulouse-Lautrec

Gustave Flaubert

Mark Twain

John Paul Getty

Finding Your Sun Sign (2020 dates)

Aries	20 March–19 April*
Taurus	20 April–20 May
Gemini	21 May–20 June
Cancer	21 June–21 July
Leo	22 July–22 August
Virgo	23 August–22 September
Libra	23 September–22 October
Scorpio	23 October–21 November
Sagittarius	22 November–20 December
Capricorn	21 December–20 January
Aquarius	21 January–18 February
Pisces	19 February–19 March

*The dates provided in this book reflect the year 2020.
Dates may vary by a day or two from year to year.